Also by Arthur V. Prosper

Stop Paying Your Credit Cards: Obtain Credit Card Debt Forgiveness Volume 1

DEBT FORGIVENESS Volume 2 WHEN CREDITORS DECIDE TO SUE

Dynamic Budgeting Techniques: Cut your expenses in half and double your income

The Simplest Path to Wealth: Turn $50,000 into $3.3 Million

The Six Million Dollar Retiree: Your roadmap to a six million dollar retirement nest egg

Living Rich & Loving It: Your guide to a rich, happy, healthy, simple and balanced life

DISCLAIMER

Notice: The information contained in this book is provided to you "AS IS" and does not constitute legal or financial advice. The advice provided is general advice only and does not take into account your own personal objectives, financial situation or needs. Consult a tax attorney or a financial professional before acting on any information provided herein. Information provided in this book is deemed reliable but is not guaranteed. Any companies, enterprises, organizations and products mentioned in this book are for reference only, have no affiliation with the author or publisher and are not specifically endorsed by the author or publisher.

All rights reserved. No part of this book may be reproduced by any means without prior permission from the author.

ABOUT THE AUTHOR

Arthur V. Prosper heads the finance department of a privately held manufacturing firm in the great state of New Jersey. Previously, he was the Vice President of Finance of the Kuoni Group and the Accounting Director of Cantel Medical. He was responsible for the financial objectives, retirement and benefit plans, investment goals and capital structures of the companies he worked for.

Arthur V. Prosper is a freelance writer, author and columnist with 30 years of experience in finance and taxation. He writes articles about the markets and finance under the header "DidoSphere, DidoSpin and Vox Populi". He is the author of several published articles in business, politics, sports and entertainment including: How We Got Here, Market Crash of 2008, Housing Bubble, The Obama Recession, Bank Stress Tests & Other Terms, Scrap Mark to Market Valuation, Recession Over, The Labyrinth of Obamacare, Bush-Obama Recession, No Different From the Rest, A Tale of Two States, NJ & VA, SEC's Case vs. GS&CO., Weak, Most Experts Agree, PIIGS: Too Big to Fail, What Causes Stock Market Fluctuations, Sluggish Recovery, Good for Investors, QE2=Printing Money, Stock Market Investors, Fasten Your Seatbelt, No Double Dip Recession, 10% Unemployment Rate, Not Enough to Derail Recovery

****
Visit the author's website: http://didosphere.com/
Author's email address: arthurvprosper@gmail.com
****

Table of Contents

Introduction 1
   PART I 2
Even financial experts can't agree 2
   PART II – Tax Comparison Tables 9
SINGLE - STANDARD DEDUCTION UNDER 65 YEARS OF AGE . 9
SINGLE - STANDARD DEDUCTION 65 YEARS OF AGE AND OLDER 12
SINGLE -ITEMIZED DEDUCTIONS REGARDLESS OF AGE 15
SINGLE - ITEMIZED DEDUCTIONS $25k in SALT deductions & $10k other, REGARDLESS OF AGE 18
MARRIED - STANDARD DEDUCTION BOTH UNDER 65 YEARS OF AGE 19
MARRIED - STANDARD DEDUCTION BOTH 65 YEARS AND OLDER 22
MARRIED - ITEMIZED DEDUCTIONS $12k in SALT deductions & $8k other, REGARDLESS OF AGE 25
MARRIED - ITEMIZED DEDUCTIONS $25k in SALT deductions & $15k other, REGARDLESS OF AGE 30
HEAD OF HOUSEHOLD - STANDARD DEDUCTION UNDER 65 YEARS OF AGE 32
HEAD OF HOUSEHOLD - STANDARD DEDUCTION 65 YEARS OF AGE AND OLDER 35
HEAD OF HOUSEHOLD - ITEMIZED DEDUCTION $12k in SALT deductions & $8k other, REGARDLESS OF AGE 38
MARRIED - STANDARD DEDUCTION BOTH UNDER 65 YEARS OF AGE, WITH 2 MINOR CHILDREN 44
MARRIED - ITEMIZED DEDUCTIONS WITH 2 MINOR CHILDREN, $25k in SALT deductions & $15k other, REGARDLESS OF AGE 46
   CONCLUSION 48

How Much Federal Income Tax Will I Pay in 2018?

The New Tax Law's winners and losers

Arthur V. Prosper

COPYRIGHT©2018 BY ARTHUR V. PROSPER * A-TEAM PUBLISHING GROUP * PO BOX 153 * PINEBROOK, NEW JERSEY 07058

COPYRIGHT AND TRADEMARK OWNERSHIP

All rights reserved. No part of this publication may be reproduced, stored in a retrieval system or transmitted by any means, electronic, mechanical, photocopying, recording, scanning or otherwise except as permitted under Section 107 or 108 of the 1976 United States Copyright Act, without the prior permission of the author and publisher. Please be aware that any unauthorized use of the contents contained herein violates copyright laws, trademark laws, the laws of privacy and publicity, and/or other regulations and statutes. All text, images and other materials provided herein are owned by **Arthur V. Prosper** unless otherwise attributed to third parties. None of the content on these materials may be copied, reproduced, distributed, downloaded, displayed, or transmitted in any form without the prior written permission of **Arthur V. Prosper**, the legal copyright owner. However, you may copy, reproduce, distribute, download, display, or transmit the content of the materials for personal, non-commercial use provided that full attribution and citation to **Arthur V. Prosper** is included and the content is not modified, and you retain all copyright and other proprietary notices contained in the content. The permission stated above is automatically rescinded if you breach any of these terms or conditions. If permission is rescinded or denied, you must immediately destroy any downloaded and/or printed content.

FBI Anti-Piracy Warning: The unauthorized reproduction or distribution of a copyrighted work is illegal. Criminal copyright infringement, including infringement without monetary gain, is investigated by the FBI and is punishable by up to five years in federal prison and a fine of $250,000.

PAPERBACK ISBN: 9781726705790
Imprint: Independently published
Cover Design by Kristjan Victorino
Printed in the United States
Printed in the United States
Author's Email Address: arthurvprosper@gmail.com

Excerpt from the book, *Living Rich & Loving It*: 53
Supplemental Disclaimer 55

****

Introduction

****

I want to thank you for purchasing the book, *"How Much Federal Income Tax Will I Pay in 2018?"* If this book helped you, your positive review would be much appreciated.

During the past year we have been inundated with so much real news as well as fake news with regard to the benefits and shortfall of the new tax law that I found it necessary to write this book to simplify the basic tax liability of each taxpayer by creating tables of various scenarios that you can apply to your own individual income tax filing situation. I have been preparing individual and corporate tax returns for 37 years but even I am confused with the information, misinformation, incomplete information and out dated information coming from many different sources. What this book expects to accomplish is to show you how much in federal individual income tax you will pay under the recently passed tax reform bill, officially known as the Tax Cuts and Jobs Act of 2017 ("TCJA") Public law no. 115-97. The final changes are shown on the link below but are always subject to modification as our legislators and IRS officials see fit:

https://www.congress.gov/bill/115th-congress/house-bill/1

The final provisions of the new tax law will change as lawmakers discover "bugs" in the way the rules and regulations were written. Refinements will be made and revisions will have to be added to "debug" the new rules and regulations. But how do the changes affect you? How much more or less will you pay in federal taxes in 2018 compared to what you paid in 2017? You will find the answer in the tables that follow.

PART I

Even financial experts can't agree

Although the IRS website indicates that they are still working on the changes to the income tax withholding tables, the comparison charts that follow accurately show how much federal income tax you would pay under the current system and how much you would pay in 2018 when the new tax law takes effect. The charts were created using the 2017 tax brackets vs. the new 2018 brackets. All you have to do is choose the table that closely resembles your own income level and filing status. Each table shows the 2017 and 2018 tax liabilities for each section. If none of the charts is applicable to your own unique situation, download either one of the books below and click on the chapter, **"How does the new tax law affect the strategies in this book?"**

The Simplest Path to Wealth
https://www.amazon.com/Simplest-Path-Wealth-Turn-Million-ebook/dp/B01KPQB0OS/ref=asap_bc?ie=UTF8

The Six Million Dollar Retiree
https://www.amazon.com/Six-Million-Dollar-Retiree-retirement-ebook/dp/B073XTL47J/ref=asap_bc?ie=UTF8

There have been many confusing discussions and opposing viewpoints as to the new tax law's winners and losers. Financial experts, economists, accountants and tax attorneys can't even agree. To add to the confusion, although the law passed, many adjustments and refinements to the bill are still being made. However, the "Total Federal Tax" shown at the bottom of each chart should not change much. The following changes were considered in creating the comparison tables. These are the basic changes that affect all taxpayers and the changes that matter most to taxpayers:

1) The elimination of the personal exemption which is $4,050 in 2017 (source IRS website: https://www.irs.gov/newsroom/in-2017-some-tax-benefits-increase-slightly-due-to-inflation-adjustments-others-are-unchanged

2) The limitation of State, local and property taxes ("SALT") to $10,000 for all filing statuses if you itemize. Source: https://www.washingtonpost.com/news/wonk/wp/2017/12/15/the-final-gop-tax-bill-is-complete-heres-what-is-in-it/?tid=a_mcntx&utm_term=.d5e0fa6bde29

3) The increase of the standard deduction for single filers from $6,350 to $12,000 and from $12,700 to $24,000 for married couples filing jointly.

4) Mortgage interest deduction is limited to $750,000 for new loans. Existing mortgages regardless of amounts will continue to be deductible.

5) The penalty for not purchasing minimum health coverage under ACA will go away beginning January 1, 2019.

6) The child tax credit for dependent children under the age of 17 will increase from $1000 to $2000. This credit is phased out as your modified adjusted gross income ("MAGI") increases. You will get $50 less in child tax credits for every $1000 or a portion thereof that you're MAGI exceeds: $200,000 for single, head of household or married filing separately. $400,000 for married filing jointly. The refundable child tax credit for the poor increased to a maximum of $1400.

7) Across the board reduction of the current tax rates. Although the final tax brackets are not final and are subject to change, the tax brackets for 2017 and 2018 as submitted in "TCJA, PL 115-97" are shown below:

	SINGLE 2017	SINGLE 2018
SINGLE	$0 - $9,324 10%	$0 - $9,524 10%
	$9,325 - $37,949 15%	$9,525 - $38,699 12%
	$37,950 - $91,899 25%	$38,700 - $59,999 22.5%
	$91,900 - $191,649 28%	$60,000 - $169,999 25.0%
	$191,650 - $416,699 33%	$170,000 - $199,999 32.5%
		$200,000 - $499,999 35%

	MARRIED 2017	MARRIED 2018
MARRIED FILING JOINTLY	$0 - $18,649	$0 - $19,049
	10%	10%
	$18,650 - $75,899	$19,050 - $77,399
	15%	12%
	$75,900 - $153,099	$77,400 - $119,999
	25%	22.5%
	$153,100 - $233,349	$120,000 - $289,999
	28%	25.0%
	$233,350 - $416,700	$290,000 - $389,999
	33%	32.5%

	HOH 2017	HOH 2018
HEAD OF HOUSEHOLD	$0 - $13,349	$0 - $13,599
	10%	10%
	$13,350 - $50,799	$13,600 - $51,799
	15%	12%
	$50,800 - $131,199	$51,800 - $59,999
	25%	22.5%
	$131,200 - $212,499	$60,000 - $169,999
	28%	25.0%
	$212,500 - $416,699	$170,000 - $199,999
	33%	25.0%
		$200,000 - $499,999
		35%

The elimination of the personal exemption of $4050 is a big hit for families with many dependents. With the new tax law, the benefit of claiming individuals that you support as dependents went away. The $4050 allowance for each dependent that you could claim in 2017 is no more. The allowance was replaced with a dependent child tax credit as explained on point 6 above and with a $500 tax credit for each child over the age of 17 and non-child dependent (parent and other qualifying relatives).

The $10,000 "SALT" limit for all filing statuses does not make sense. I predict that this is one provision that will be revised during tax year 2018 before the tax filing deadline of April 15, 2019. This provision of the tax bill was rushed through. Not enough thought was given as to why a single tax payer is entitled to the same $10,000 deduction as a married couple filing jointly or head of a household.

Certain states such as New York, New Jersey and Connecticut are drafting proposals to treat the property taxes, which were severely limited under this new tax law, as charitable contributions to the state. Charitable contributions will continue to be deductible under the new law although limited to 60% of the taxpayer's MAGI. Other significant provisions of the new law are:

- Charitable contributions and student loan interest will continue to be deductible.

- The rules on elective deferrals, IRA, 401k and Roth IRA and 401k have not changed much. Contribution limits for 2018 stayed the same. However, the MAGI phase out for Roth contributions now starts at $120,000 for single filers and $189,000 for joint filers. The only change on the conversion rules from traditional IRA into Roth is that the 2-year deferral option went away. The amount converted must now be reported as ordinary income in the year of conversion instead of over a 2-year period. Recharacterization rules for conversions have not changed.

- Alimony payments are no longer deductible.

- Moving expenses are limited to U.S. Military personnel.

- Medical expenses that exceed 7.5% of your MAGI are still deductible. In 2017 the limit is 10% of MAGI for taxpayers who are under age 65. Therefore, this new lower threshold is favorable to taxpayers.

- Miscellaneous Itemized Deductions Subject to the 2% Floor, such as unreimbursed employee expenses, home office deduction, tax preparation fees, advisory investment fees, etc. will no longer be deductible.

- Estate tax exemption doubles to $11.2 million for singles and $22.4 million for couples filing jointly.

- Alternative Minimum Tax – Exemption increased from $54,300 to $70,300 for singles and from $84,500 to $109,400 for joint filers.

- Bike Credit - $20 per month deduction for people who bike to work.

For the average taxpayer like you and me, what matters most is how these changes really translate into what you have to pay in taxes. How does my tax liability in 2017 under the current system compare to 2018 under the new tax law? Will I pay more or less and how much? The comparison tables that follow should answer your questions.

PART II – Tax Comparison Tables

SINGLE - STANDARD DEDUCTION UNDER 65 YEARS OF AGE

SINGLE - STANDARD DEDUCTION UNDER 65 YEARS OF AGE	SINGLE 2017	SINGLE 2018
FEDERAL WAGES (NET OF ELECTIVE DEFERRAL)	50000	50000
PERSONAL EXEMPTION	4050	0
STANDARD DEDUCTION	6350	12000
TOTAL DEDUCTIONS	10400	12000
TAXABLE INCOME	39600	38000
TAX RATES	$0 - $9,324 10.0%	$0 - $9,524 10.0%
	$9,325 - $37,949 15.0%	$9,525 - $38,699 12.0%
	$37,950 - $91,899 25.0%	$38,700 - $59,999 22.5%
	$91,900 - $191,649 28.0%	$60,000 - $169,999 25.0%
	$191,650 - $416,699 33.0%	$170,000 - $199,999 32.5%
		$200,000 - $499,999 35.0%
TOTAL FEDERAL TAX	5639	4370

SINGLE - STANDARD DEDUCTION UNDER 65 YEARS OF AGE	SINGLE 2017	SINGLE 2018
FEDERAL WAGES (NET OF ELECTIVE DEFERRAL)	75000	75000
PERSONAL EXEMPTION	4050	0
STANDARD DEDUCTION	6350	12000
TOTAL DEDUCTIONS	10400	12000
TAXABLE INCOME	64600	63000
TAX RATES	$0 - $9,324 10.0% $9,325 - $37,949 15.0% $37,950 - $91,899 25.0% $91,900 - $191,649 28.0% $191,650 - $416,699 33.0%	$0 - $9,524 10.0% $9,525 - $38,699 12.0% $38,700 - $59,999 22.5% $60,000 - $169,999 25.0% $170,000 - $199,999 32.5% $200,000 - $499,999 35.0%
TOTAL FEDERAL TAX	11890	9996

SINGLE - STANDARD DEDUCTION UNDER 65 YEARS OF AGE	SINGLE 2017	SINGLE 2018
FEDERAL WAGES (NET OF ELECTIVE DEFERRAL)	100000	100000
PERSONAL EXEMPTION	4050	0
STANDARD DEDUCTION	6350	12000
TOTAL DEDUCTIONS	10400	12000
TAXABLE INCOME	89600	88000
TAX RATES	$0 - $9,324	$0 - $9,524
	10.0%	10.0%
	$9,325 - $37,949	$9,525 - $38,699
	15.0%	12.0%
	$37,950 - $91,899	$38,700 - $59,999
	25.0%	22.5%
	$91,900 - $191,649	$60,000 - $169,999
	28.0%	25.0%
	$191,650 - $416,699	$170,000 - $199,999
	33.0%	32.5%
		$200,000 - $499,999
		35.0%
TOTAL FEDERAL TAX	18140	16246

SINGLE - STANDARD DEDUCTION 65 YEARS OF AGE AND OLDER

SINGLE - STANDARD DEDUCTION 65 YEARS OF AGE AND OLDER	SINGLE 2017	SINGLE 2018
FEDERAL WAGES (NET OF ELECTIVE DEFERRAL)	50000	50000
PERSONAL EXEMPTION	4050	0
STANDARD DEDUCTION	7900	13250
TOTAL DEDUCTIONS	11950	13250
TAXABLE INCOME	38050	36750
TAX RATES	$0 - $9,324　10.0% $9,325 - $37,949　15.0% $37,950 - $91,899　25.0% $91,900 - $191,649　28.0% $191,650 - $416,699　33.0%	$0 - $9,524　10.0% $9,525 - $38,699　12.0% $38,700 - $59,999　22.5% $60,000 - $169,999　25.0% $170,000 - $199,999　32.5% $200,000 - $499,999　35.0%
TOTAL FEDERAL TAX	5251	4220

SINGLE - STANDARD DEDUCTION 65 YEARS OF AGE AND OLDER	SINGLE 2017	SINGLE 2018
FEDERAL WAGES (NET OF ELECTIVE DEFERRAL)	75000	75000
PERSONAL EXEMPTION	4050	0
STANDARD DEDUCTION	7900	13250
TOTAL DEDUCTIONS	11950	13250
TAXABLE INCOME	63050	61750
TAX RATES	$0 - $9,324 10.0% $9,325 - $37,949 15.0% $37,950 - $91,899 25.0% $91,900 - $191,649 28.0% $191,650 - $416,699 33.0%	$0 - $9,524 10.0% $9,525 - $38,699 12.0% $38,700 - $59,999 22.5% $60,000 - $169,999 25.0% $170,000 - $199,999 32.5% $200,000 - $499,999 35.0%
TOTAL FEDERAL TAX	11501	9640

SINGLE - STANDARD DEDUCTION 65 YEARS OF AGE AND OLDER	SINGLE 2017	SINGLE 2018
FEDERAL WAGES (NET OF ELECTIVE DEFERRAL)	100000	100000
PERSONAL EXEMPTION	4050	0
STANDARD DEDUCTION	7900	13250
TOTAL DEDUCTIONS	11950	13250
TAXABLE INCOME	88050	86750
TAX RATES	$0 - $9,324 10.0% $9,325 - $37,949 15.0% $37,950 - $91,899 25.0% $91,900 - $191,649 28.0% $191,650 - $416,699 33.0%	$0 - $9,524 10.0% $9,525 - $38,699 12.0% $38,700 - $59,999 22.5% $60,000 - $169,999 25.0% $170,000 - $199,999 32.5% $200,000 - $499,999 35.0%
TOTAL FEDERAL TAX	17751	15934

SINGLE - ITEMIZED DEDUCTIONS REGARDLESS OF AGE

SINGLE - ITEMIZED DEDUCTIONS REGARDLESS OF AGE	SINGLE 2017	SINGLE 2018
FEDERAL WAGES (NET OF ELECTIVE DEFERRAL)	50000	50000
PERSONAL EXEMPTION	4050	0
STATE & LOCAL & PROPERTY TAX ("SALT")	12000	10000
MORTGAGE INTEREST, CHARITY, MEDICAL & TUITION DEDUCTION	8000	8000
THE HIGHER OF:		
ITEMIZED DEDUCTIONS & EXEMPTION or	24050	18000
STANDARD DEDUCTIONS		12000
TAXABLE INCOME	25950	32000
TAX RATES	$0 - $9,324 10.0%	$0 - $9,524 10.0%
	$9,325 - $37,949 15.0%	$9,525 - $38,699 12.0%
	$37,950 - $91,899 25.0%	$38,700 - $59,999 22.5%
	$91,900 - $191,649 28.0%	$60,000 - $169,999 25.0%
	$191,650 - $416,699 33.0%	$170,000 - $199,999 32.5%
		$200,000 - $499,999 35.0%
TOTAL FEDERAL TAX	**3426**	**3650**

SINGLE - ITEMIZED DEDUCTIONS REGARDLESS OF AGE	SINGLE 2017	SINGLE 2018
FEDERAL WAGES (NET OF ELECTIVE DEFERRAL)	75000	75000
PERSONAL EXEMPTION	4050	0
STATE & LOCAL & PROPERTY TAX ("SALT")	12000	10000
MORTGAGE INTEREST, CHARITY, MEDICAL & TUITION DEDUCTION	8000	8000
The higher of:		
ITEMIZED DEDUCTIONS & EXEMPTION or	24050	18000
STANDARD DEDUCTIONS		12000
TAXABLE INCOME	50950	57000
TAX RATES	$0 - $9,324 10.0% $9,325 - $37,949 15.0% $37,950 - $91,899 25.0% $91,900 - $191,649 28.0% $191,650 - $416,699 33.0%	$0 - $9,524 10.0% $9,525 - $38,699 12.0% $38,700 - $59,999 22.5% $60,000 - $169,999 25.0% $170,000 - $199,999 32.5% $200,000 - $499,999 35.0%
TOTAL FEDERAL TAX	8476	8571

SINGLE - ITEMIZED DEDUCTIONS REGARDLESS OF AGE	SINGLE 2017	SINGLE 2018
FEDERAL WAGES (NET OF ELECTIVE DEFERRAL)	100000	100000
PERSONAL EXEMPTION	4050	0
STATE & LOCAL & PROPERTY TAX ("SALT")	12000	10000
MORTGAGE INTEREST, CHARITY, MEDICAL & TUITION DEDUCTION	8000	8000
THE HIGHER OF:		
ITEMIZED DEDUCTIONS & EXEMPTION or	24050	18000
STANDARD DEDUCTIONS		12000
TAXABLE INCOME	75950	82000
TAX RATES	$0 - $9,324	$0 - $9,524
	10.0%	10.0%
	$9,325 - $37,949	$9,525 - $38,699
	15.0%	12.0%
	$37,950 - $91,899	$38,700 - $59,999
	25.0%	22.5%
	$91,900 - $191,649	$60,000 - $169,999
	28.0%	25.0%
	$191,650 - $416,699	$170,000 - $199,999
	33.0%	32.5%
		$200,000 - $499,999
		35.0%
TOTAL FEDERAL TAX	14726	14746

SINGLE - ITEMIZED DEDUCTIONS $25k in SALT deductions & $10k other, REGARDLESS OF AGE

SINGLE - ITEMIZED DEDUCTIONS $25k in SALT deductions & $10k other REGARDLESS OF AGE	SINGLE 2017	SINGLE 2018
FEDERAL WAGES (NET OF ELECTIVE DEFERRAL)	100,000	100,000
PERSONAL EXEMPTION	4,050	-
STATE & LOCAL & PROPERTY TAX ("SALT")	25,000	10,000
MORTGAGE INTEREST, CHARITY, MEDICAL & TUITION DEDUCTION	10,000	10,000
The higher of:		
ITEMIZED DEDUCTIONS & EXEMPTION or	39,050	20,000
STANDARD DEDUCTIONS		12,000
TAXABLE INCOME	60,950	80,000
TAX RATES	$0 - $9,324	$0 - $9,524
	10%	10%
	$9,325 - $37,949	$9,525 - $38,699
	15%	12%
	$37,950 - $91,899	$38,700 - $59,999
	25%	22.5%
	$91,900 - $191,649	$60,000 - $169,999
	28%	25.0%
	$191,650 - $416,699	$170,000 - $199,999
	33%	32.5%
		$200,000 - $499,999
		35%
TOTAL FEDERAL TAX	10,976	14,246

MARRIED - STANDARD DEDUCTION BOTH UNDER 65 YEARS OF AGE

MARRIED - STANDARD DEDUCTION BOTH UNDER 65 YEARS OF AGE	MARRIED 2017	MARRIED 2018
FEDERAL WAGES (NET OF ELECTIVE DEFERRAL)	80000	80000
PERSONAL EXEMPTION	8100	0
STANDARD DEDUCTION	12700	24000
TOTAL DEDUCTIONS	20800	24000
TAXABLE INCOME	59200	56000
TAX RATES	$0 - $18,649	$0 - $19,049
	10.0%	10.0%
	$18,650 - $75,899	$19,050 - $77,399
	15.0%	12.0%
	$75,900 - $153,099	$77,400 - $119,999
	25.0%	22.5%
	$153,100 - $233,349	$120,000 - $289,999
	28.0%	25.0%
	$233,350 - $416,700	$290,000 - $389,999
	33.0%	32.5%
TOTAL FEDERAL TAX	7948	6339

MARRIED - STANDARD DEDUCTION BOTH UNDER 65 YEARS OF AGE	MARRIED 2017	MARRIED 2018
FEDERAL WAGES (NET OF ELECTIVE DEFERRAL)	100000	100000
PERSONAL EXEMPTION	8100	0
STANDARD DEDUCTION	12700	24000
TOTAL DEDUCTIONS	20800	24000
TAXABLE INCOME	79200	76000
TAX RATES	$0 - $18,649　10.0% $18,650 - $75,899　15.0% $75,900 - $153,099　25.0% $153,100 - $233,349　28.0% $233,350 - $416,700　33.0%	$0 - $19,049　10.0% $19,050 - $77,399　12.0% $77,400 - $119,999　22.5% $120,000 - $289,999　25.0% $290,000 - $389,999　32.5%
TOTAL FEDERAL TAX	11278	8739

MARRIED - STANDARD DEDUCTION BOTH UNDER 65 YEARS OF AGE	MARRIED 2017	MARRIED 2018
FEDERAL WAGES (NET OF ELECTIVE DEFERRAL)	125000	125000
PERSONAL EXEMPTION	8100	0
STANDARD DEDUCTION	12700	24000
TOTAL DEDUCTIONS	20800	24000
TAXABLE INCOME	104200	101000
TAX RATES	$0 - $18,649 10.0%	$0 - $19,049 10.0%
	$18,650 - $75,899 15.0%	$19,050 - $77,399 12.0%
	$75,900 - $153,099 25.0%	$77,400 - $119,999 22.5%
	$153,100 - $233,349 28.0%	$120,000 - $289,999 25.0%
	$233,350 - $416,700 33.0%	$290,000 - $389,999 32.5%
TOTAL FEDERAL TAX	17528	14217

MARRIED - STANDARD DEDUCTION BOTH 65 YEARS AND OLDER

MARRIED - STANDARD DEDUCTION BOTH 65 YEARS AND OLDER	MARRIED 2017	MARRIED 2018
FEDERAL WAGES (NET OF ELECTIVE DEFERRAL)	80000	80000
PERSONAL EXEMPTION	8100	0
STANDARD DEDUCTION	15200	26600
TOTAL DEDUCTIONS	23300	26600
TAXABLE INCOME	56700	53400
TAX RATES	$0 - $18,649 10.0% $18,650 - $75,899 15.0% $75,900 - $153,099 25.0% $153,100 - $233,349 28.0% $233,350 - $416,700 33.0%	$0 - $19,049 10.0% $19,050 - $77,399 12.0% $77,400 - $119,999 22.5% $120,000 - $289,999 25.0% $290,000 - $389,999 32.5%
TOTAL FEDERAL TAX	7573	6027

MARRIED - STANDARD DEDUCTION BOTH 65 YEARS AND OLDER	MARRIED 2017	MARRIED 2018
FEDERAL WAGES (NET OF ELECTIVE DEFERRAL)	100000	100000
PERSONAL EXEMPTION	8100	0
STANDARD DEDUCTION	15200	26600
TOTAL DEDUCTIONS	23300	26600
TAXABLE INCOME	76700	73400
TAX RATES	$0 - $18,649　10.0%	$0 - $19,049　10.0%
	$18,650 - $75,899　15.0%	$19,050 - $77,399　12.0%
	$75,900 - $153,099　25.0%	$77,400 - $119,999　22.5%
	$153,100 - $233,349　28.0%	$120,000 - $289,999　25.0%
	$233,350 - $416,700　33.0%	$290,000 - $389,999　32.5%
TOTAL FEDERAL TAX	10653	8427

MARRIED - STANDARD DEDUCTION BOTH 65 YEARS AND OLDER	MARRIED 2017	MARRIED 2018
FEDERAL WAGES (NET OF ELECTIVE DEFERRAL)	125000	125000
PERSONAL EXEMPTION	8100	0
STANDARD DEDUCTION	15200	26600
TOTAL DEDUCTIONS	23300	26600
TAXABLE INCOME	101700	98400
TAX RATES	$0 - $18,649 10.0% $18,650 - $75,899 15.0% $75,900 - $153,099 25.0% $153,100 - $233,349 28.0% $233,350 - $416,700 33.0%	$0 - $19,049 10.0% $19,050 - $77,399 12.0% $77,400 - $119,999 22.5% $120,000 - $289,999 25.0% $290,000 - $389,999 32.5%
TOTAL FEDERAL TAX	16903	13632

MARRIED - ITEMIZED DEDUCTIONS $12k in SALT deductions & $8k other, REGARDLESS OF AGE

MARRIED - ITEMIZED DEDUCTIONS $12k in SALT deductions & $8k other REGARDLESS OF AGE	MARRIED 2017	MARRIED 2018
FEDERAL WAGES (NET OF ELECTIVE DEFERRAL)	80000	80000
PERSONAL EXEMPTION	8100	0
STATE & LOCAL & PROPERTY TAX ("SALT")	12000	10000
MORTGAGE INTEREST, CHARITY, MEDICAL & TUITION DEDUCTION	8000	8000
The higher of:		
ITEMIZED DEDUCTIONS & EXEMPTION or	28100	18000
STANDARD DEDUCTIONS		24000
TAXABLE INCOME	51900	56000
TAX RATES	$0 - $18,649	$0 - $19,049
	10.0%	10.0%

	$18,650 - $75,899	$19,050 - $77,399
	15.0%	12.0%
	$75,900 - $153,099	$77,400 - $119,999
	25.0%	22.5%
	$153,100 - $233,349	$120,000 - $289,999
	28.0%	25.0%
	$233,350 - $416,700	$290,000 - $389,999
	33.0%	32.5%
TOTAL FEDERAL TAX	**6853**	**6339**

	MARRIED 2017	MARRIED 2018
MARRIED - ITEMIZED DEDUCTIONS $12k in SALT deductions & $8k other REGARDLESS OF AGE		
FEDERAL WAGES (NET OF ELECTIVE DEFERRAL)	100000	100000
PERSONAL EXEMPTION	8100	0
STATE & LOCAL & PROPERTY TAX ("SALT")	12000	10000
MORTGAGE INTEREST, CHARITY, MEDICAL & TUITION DEDUCTION	8000	8000
The higher of:		
ITEMIZED DEDUCTIONS & EXEMPTION or	28100	18000
STANDARD DEDUCTIONS		24000
TAXABLE INCOME	71900	76000
TAX RATES	$0 - $18,649	$0 - $19,049
	10.0%	10.0%
	$18,650 - $75,899	$19,050 - $77,399
	15.0%	12.0%
	$75,900 - $153,099	$77,400 - $119,999
	25.0%	22.5%
	$153,100 - $233,349	$120,000 - $289,999
	28.0%	25.0%
	$233,350 - $416,700	$290,000 - $389,999
	33.0%	32.5%
TOTAL FEDERAL TAX	9853	8739

MARRIED - ITEMIZED DEDUCTIONS $12k in SALT deductions & $8k other REGARDLESS OF AGE	MARRIED 2017	MARRIED 2018
FEDERAL WAGES (NET OF ELECTIVE DEFERRAL)	125000	125000
PERSONAL EXEMPTION	8100	0
STATE & LOCAL & PROPERTY TAX ("SALT")	12000	10000
MORTGAGE INTEREST, CHARITY, MEDICAL & TUITION DEDUCTION	8000	8000
The higher of: ITEMIZED DEDUCTIONS & EXEMPTION or	28100	18000
STANDARD DEDUCTIONS		24000
TAXABLE INCOME	96900	101000

TAX RATES	$0 - $18,649	$0 - $19,049
	10.0%	10.0%
	$18,650 - $75,899	$19,050 - $77,399
	15.0%	12.0%
	$75,900 - $153,099	$77,400 - $119,999
	25.0%	22.5%
	$153,100 -$233,349	$120,000 -$289,999
	28.0%	25.0%
	$233,350 -$416,700	$290,000 -$389,999
	33.0%	32.5%
TOTAL FEDERAL TAX	**15703**	**14217**

MARRIED - ITEMIZED DEDUCTIONS $25k in SALT deductions & $15k other, REGARDLESS OF AGE

MARRIED - ITEMIZED DEDUCTIONS $25k in SALT deductions & $15k other REGARDLESS OF AGE	MARRIED 2017	MARRIED 2018
FEDERAL WAGES (NET OF ELECTIVE DEFERRAL)	125000	125000
PERSONAL EXEMPTION	8100	0
STATE & LOCAL & PROPERTY TAX ("SALT")	25000	10000
MORTGAGE INTEREST, CHARITY, MEDICAL & TUITION DEDUCTION	15000	15000
The higher of: ITEMIZED DEDUCTIONS & EXEMPTION or	48100	25000
STANDARD DEDUCTIONS		24000

TAXABLE INCOME	76900	100000
TAX RATES	$0 - $18,649 10.0%	$0 - $19,049 10.0%
	$18,650 - $75,899 15.0%	$19,050 - $77,399 12.0%
	$75,900 - $153,099 25.0%	$77,400 - $119,999 22.5%
	$153,100 - $233,349 28.0%	$120,000 - $289,999 25.0%
	$233,350 - $416,700 33.0%	$290,000 - $389,999 32.5%
TOTAL FEDERAL TAX	**10703**	**13992**

HEAD OF HOUSEHOLD - STANDARD DEDUCTION UNDER 65 YEARS OF AGE

HEAD OF HOUSEHOLD - STANDARD DEDUCTION UNDER 65 YEARS OF AGE	HOH 2017	HOH 2018
FEDERAL WAGES (NET OF ELECTIVE DEFERRAL)	50000	50000
PERSONAL EXEMPTION	4050	0
STANDARD DEDUCTIONS	9350	18000
TOTAL DEDUCTIONS	13400	18000
TAXABLE INCOME	36600	32000
TAX RATES	$0 - $13,349 10.0%	$0 - $13,599 10.0%
	$13,350 - $50,799 15.0%	$13,600 - $51,799 12.0%
	$50,800 - $131,199 25.0%	$51,800 - $59,999 22.5%
	$131,200 - $212,499 28.0%	$60,000 - $169,999 25.0%
	$212,500 - $416,699 33.0%	$170,000 - $199,999 25.0%
		$200,000 - $499,999 35.0%
TOTAL FEDERAL TAX	4823	3568

HEAD OF HOUSEHOLD - STANDARD DEDUCTION UNDER 65 YEARS OF AGE	HOH 2017	HOH 2018
FEDERAL WAGES (NET OF ELECTIVE DEFERRAL)	75000	75000
PERSONAL EXEMPTION	4050	0
STANDARD DEDUCTIONS	9350	18000
TOTAL DEDUCTIONS	13400	18000
TAXABLE INCOME	61600	57000
TAX RATES	$0 - $13,349 10.0%	$0 - $13,599 10.0%
	$13,350 - $50,799 15.0%	$13,600 - $51,799 12.0%
	$50,800 - $131,199 25.0%	$51,800 - $59,999 22.5%
	$131,200 - $212,499 28.0%	$60,000 - $169,999 25.0%
	$212,500 - $416,699 33.0%	$170,000 - $199,999 25.0%
		$200,000 - $499,999 35.0%
TOTAL FEDERAL TAX	8573	7114

HEAD OF HOUSEHOLD - STANDARD DEDUCTION UNDER 65 YEARS OF AGE	HOH 2017	HOH 2018
FEDERAL WAGES (NET OF ELECTIVE DEFERRAL)	100000	100000
PERSONAL EXEMPTION	4050	0
STANDARD DEDUCTIONS	9350	18000
TOTAL DEDUCTIONS	13400	18000
TAXABLE INCOME	86600	82000
TAX RATES	$0 - $13,349 10.0%	$0 - $13,599 10.0%
	$13,350 - $50,799 15.0%	$13,600 - $51,799 12.0%
	$50,800 - $131,199 25.0%	$51,800 - $59,999 22.5%
	$131,200 - $212,499 28.0%	$60,000 - $169,999 25.0%
	$212,500 - $416,699 33.0%	$170,000 - $199,999 25.0%
		$200,000 - $499,999 35.0%
TOTAL FEDERAL TAX	15903	12739

HEAD OF HOUSEHOLD - STANDARD DEDUCTION 65 YEARS OF AGE AND OLDER

HEAD OF HOUSEHOLD - STANDARD DEDUCTION 65 YEARS OF AGE AND OLDER	HOH 2017	HOH 2018
FEDERAL WAGES (NET OF ELECTIVE DEFERRAL)	50000	50000
PERSONAL EXEMPTION	4050	0
STANDARD DEDUCTIONS	10900	19550
TOTAL DEDUCTIONS	14950	19550
TAXABLE INCOME	35050	30450
TAX RATES	$0 - $13,349	$0 - $13,599
	10.0%	10.0%
	$13,350 - $50,799	$13,600 - $51,799
	15.0%	12.0%
	$50,800 - $131,199	$51,800 - $59,999
	25.0%	22.5%
	$131,200 - $212,499	$60,000 - $169,999
	28.0%	25.0%
	$212,500 - $416,699	$170,000 - $199,999
	33.0%	25.0%
		$200,000 - $499,999
		35.0%
TOTAL FEDERAL TAX	4590	3382

HEAD OF HOUSEHOLD - STANDARD DEDUCTION 65 YEARS OF AGE AND OLDER	HOH 2017	HOH 2018
FEDERAL WAGES (NET OF ELECTIVE DEFERRAL)	75000	75000
PERSONAL EXEMPTION	4050	0
STANDARD DEDUCTIONS	10900	19550
TOTAL DEDUCTIONS	14950	19550
TAXABLE INCOME	60050	55450
TAX RATES	$0 - $13,349	$0 - $13,599
	10.0%	10.0%
	$13,350 - $50,799	$13,600 - $51,799
	15.0%	12.0%
	$50,800 - $131,199	$51,800 - $59,999
	25.0%	22.5%
	$131,200 - $212,499	$60,000 - $169,999
	28.0%	25.0%
	$212,500 - $416,699	$170,000 - $199,999
	33.0%	25.0%
		$200,000 - $499,999
		35.0%
TOTAL FEDERAL TAX	8340	6765

HEAD OF HOUSEHOLD - STANDARD DEDUCTION 65 YEARS OF AGE AND OLDER	HOH 2017	HOH 2018
FEDERAL WAGES (NET OF ELECTIVE DEFERRAL)	100000	100000
PERSONAL EXEMPTION	4050	0
STANDARD DEDUCTIONS	10900	19550
TOTAL DEDUCTIONS	14950	19550
TAXABLE INCOME	85050	80450
TAX RATES	$0 - $13,349	$0 - $13,599
	10.0%	10.0%
	$13,350 - $50,799	$13,600 - $51,799
	15.0%	12.0%
	$50,800 - $131,199	$51,800 - $59,999
	25.0%	22.5%
	$131,200 - $212,499	$60,000 - $169,999
	28.0%	25.0%
	$212,500 -$416,699	$170,000 -$199,999
	33.0%	25.0%
		$200,000 -$499,999
		35.0%
TOTAL FEDERAL TAX	155515	12390

HEAD OF HOUSEHOLD - ITEMIZED DEDUCTION
$12k in SALT deductions & $8k other, REGARDLESS OF AGE

HEAD OF HOUSEHOLD – ITEMIZED DEDUCTION $12k in SALT deductions & $8k other REGARDLESS OF AGE	HOH 2017	HOH 2018
FEDERAL WAGES (NET OF ELECTIVE DEFERRAL)	50000	50000
PERSONAL EXEMPTION	4050	0
STATE & LOCAL & PROPERTY TAX ("SALT")	12000	10000
MORTGAGE INTEREST, CHARITY,		
MEDICAL & TUITION DEDUCTION	8000	8000

The higher of:		
ITEMIZED DEDUCTIONS & EXEMPTION or	24050	18000
STANDARD DEDUCTIONS		18000
TAXABLE INCOME	25950	32000
TAX RATES	$0 - $13,349	$0 - $13,599
	10.00%	10.00%
	$13,350 - $50,799	$13,600 - $51,799
	15.00%	12.00%
	$50,800 - $131,199	$51,800 - $59,999
	25.00%	22.50%
	$131,200 - $212,499	$60,000 - $169,999
	28.00%	25.00%
	$212,500 - $416,699	$170,000 - $199,999
	33.00%	25.00%
		$200,000 - $499,999
		35.00%
TOTAL FEDERAL TAX	3225	3568

HEAD OF HOUSEHOLD – ITEMIZED DEDUCTION $12k in SALT deductions & $8k other REGARDLESS OF AGE	HOH 2017	HOH 2018
FEDERAL WAGES (NET OF ELECTIVE DEFERRAL)	75000	75000
PERSONAL EXEMPTION	4050	0
STATE & LOCAL & PROPERTY TAX ("SALT")	12000	10000
MORTGAGE INTEREST, CHARITY,		
MEDICAL & TUITION DEDUCTION	8000	8000
The higher of:		

ITEMIZED DEDUCTIONS & EXEMPTION or	24050	18000
STANDARD DEDUCTIONS		18000
TAXABLE INCOME	50950	57000
TAX RATES	$0 - $13,349	$0 - $13,599
	10.00%	10.00%
	$13,350 - $50,799	$13,600 - $51,799
	15.00%	12.00%
	$50,800 - $131,199	$51,800 - $59,999
	25.00%	22.50%
	$131,200 -$212,499	$60,000 - $169,999
	28.00%	25.00%
	$212,500 -$416,699	$170,000 -$199,999
	33.00%	25.00%
		$200,000 -$499,999
		35.00%
TOTAL FEDERAL TAX	6990	7114

	HOH	HOH
HEAD OF HOUSEHOLD – ITEMIZED DEDUCTION $12k in SALT deductions & $8k other REGARDLESS OF AGE	2017	2018
FEDERAL WAGES (NET OF ELECTIVE DEFERRAL)	100000	100000
PERSONAL EXEMPTION	4050	0
STATE & LOCAL & PROPERTY TAX ("SALT")	12000	10000
MORTGAGE INTEREST, CHARITY,		
MEDICAL & TUITION DEDUCTION	8000	8000
The higher of:		

ITEMIZED DEDUCTIONS & EXEMPTION or	24050	18000
STANDARD DEDUCTIONS		18000
TAXABLE INCOME	75950	82000
TAX RATES	$0 - $13,349	$0 - $13,599
	10.00%	10.00%
	$13,350 - $50,799	$13,600 - $51,799
	15.00%	12.00%
	$50,800 - $131,199	$51,800 - $59,999
	25.00%	22.50%
	$131,200 - $212,499	$60,000 - $169,999
	28.00%	25.00%
	$212,500 - $416,699	$170,000 - $199,999
	33.00%	25.00%
		$200,000 - $499,999
		35.00%
TOTAL FEDERAL TAX	**13240**	**13289**

MARRIED - STANDARD DEDUCTION BOTH UNDER 65 YEARS OF AGE, WITH 2 MINOR CHILDREN

MARRIED - STANDARD DEDUCTION BOTH UNDER 65 YEARS OF AGE WITH 2 CHILDREN UNDER 17	MARRIED 2017	MARRIED 2018
FEDERAL WAGES (NET OF ELECTIVE DEFERRAL)	120000	120000
PERSONAL EXEMPTION	16200	0
STANDARD DEDUCTION	12700	24000
TOTAL DEDUCTIONS	28900	24000
TAXABLE INCOME	91100	96000
TAX RATES	$0 - $18,649 10.0%	$0 - $19,049 10.0%
	$18,650 - $75,899 15.0%	$19,050 - $77,399 12.0%
	$75,900 - $153,099 25.0%	$77,400 - $119,999 22.5%

	$153,100-$233,349	$120,000 - $289,999
	28.0%	25.0%
	$233,350 - $416,700	$290,000 - $389,999
	33.0%	32.5%
FEDERAL TAX BEFORE CREDITS	14253	13092
CHILD CREDIT	-2000	-4000
TOTAL FEDERAL TAX	**12253**	**9092**

MARRIED - ITEMIZED DEDUCTIONS WITH 2 MINOR CHILDREN, $25k in SALT deductions & $15k other, REGARDLESS OF AGE

MARRIED - ITEMIZED DEDUCTIONS WITH 2 CHILDREN UNDER 17	MARRIED	MARRIED
$25k in SALT deductions & $15k other		
REGARDLESS OF AGE	2017	2018
FEDERAL WAGES (NET OF ELECTIVE DEFERRAL)	120000	120000
PERSONAL EXEMPTION	16200	0
STATE & LOCAL & PROPERTY TAX ("SALT")	25000	10000
MORTGAGE INTEREST, CHARITY,		
MEDICAL & TUITION DEDUCTION	15000	15000

The higher of:		
ITEMIZED DEDUCTIONS & EXEMPTION or	56200	25000
STANDARD DEDUCTIONS		24000
TAXABLE INCOME	63800	95000
TAX RATES	$0 - $18,649	$0 - $19,049
	10.0%	10.0%
	$18,650 - $75,899	$19,050 - $77,399
	15.0%	12.0%
	$75,900 - $153,099	$77,400 - $119,999
	25.0%	22.5%
	$153,100 - $233,349	$120,000 - $289,999
	28.0%	25.0%
	$233,350 - $416,700	$290,000 - $389,999
	33.0%	32.5%
FEDERAL TAX BEFORE CREDITS	8638	12867
CHILD CREDIT	-2000	-4000
TOTAL FEDERAL TAX	**6638**	**8867**

CONCLUSION

The passage of The tax reform bill into law, now officially known as the Tax Cuts and Jobs Act of 2017 ("TCJA") Public law no. 115-97, only proves my point that we should NOT focus too much on taxes when formulating an investment and retirement strategy. Making long term investment and retirement plans based on taxation is an exercise in futility because future tax rates and other tax changes are unknowable. The pendulum swings the other way every 8 years. The tax cuts in this recently passed TCJA will expire in 2025. If a Democrat wins back the White House and the Democrats take back the House and Senate, it is almost certain the Trump Tax Cuts will be allowed to expire and the tax rates will revert back to the 2017 tax brackets. Moreover, tax increases are likely when Democrats are back in power. That's not a political statement. It's just a fact of life.

There are so many variables in your own personal savings and investment situation and idiosyncrasies in the way you manage your life. How taxes will affect you in the future is unknowable. Continue to build your wealth and plan for your retirement by following the investment and retirement strategies in the books listed below. There are more important things to worry about than taxes. The figures shown under chapter, "DON'T FOCUS ON TAXES" clearly prove that there is no such thing as "Tax Free-retirement" and there is no advantage in paying the taxes now rather than in the future. There may not be an advantage in buying life insurance as an alternative to your retirement account as an inheritance to leave your beneficiaries.

Download the following books for sound investment and retirement advice:

The Simplest Path to Wealth
https://www.amazon.com/Simplest-Path-Wealth-Turn-Million-ebook/dp/B01KPQB0OS/ref=asap_bc?ie=UTF8

The Six Million Dollar Retiree
https://www.amazon.com/Six-Million-Dollar-Retiree-retirement-ebook/dp/B073XTL47J/ref=asap_bc?ie=UTF8

Dynamic Budgeting Techniques: Cut your expenses in half and double your income
https://www.amazon.com/Dynamic-Budgeting-Techniques-expenses-double-ebook/dp/B01LZA9O3W/ref=asap_bc?ie=UTF8

****

If this book helped you, your positive Amazon review would be much appreciated.
****

If you have questions or comments, VISIT THE AUTHOR'S WEBSITE and click "Ask DidoSphere":
http://didosphere.com/contact/
http://didosphere.com/
****

Living Rich & Loving It

Learn more about the subjects below from the author's new book, https://www.amazon.com/Living-Rich-Loving-healthy-balanced-ebook/dp/B01GORIB4Y/ref=sr_1_3?s=digital-text&ie=UTF8&qid=1471625403&sr=1-3&keywords=didosphere

- **Find a job you love** – If you cannot wait to get up and get to work every morning, then you have found the job you love. Otherwise, you need to read this chapter and the chapter, "Increase Your Income with these Ideas".

- **Personal Insurance** – Which is better, whole life or term insurance? How much insurance do you need? The answer may surprise you.

- **Budgeting made easy** - Follow the sample and simple budget in the book and you will always have a monthly surplus.

- **Never buy Veblen Goods** – the savings will amaze you.

- **Shop around for everything** – if you are struggling to make ends meet, this chapter will show you why. Learn how to save more and spend less.

- **How to purchase your primary residence** – Pros and cons of owning vs. renting. The analysis chart shows the clear winner which will surprise you.

- **Good debt, bad debt** – when borrowing makes sense. Analysis table proves that some debts are good.

- Do Not Take Unnecessary Risks, Don't Do Anything Stupid – this chapter shows that stupidity is the great equalizer in life. Doing any of the things on the list may change your life or worse may end your life in the blink of an eye.

- Never invest in a rental property – this chapter tells you why it is not worth being an absentee landlord.

- Never keep an emergency fund – the analysis chart shows you why and the answer will astound you.

- No Double Taxation on 401k Loans – never ever listen to Suze Orman that 401k loans are taxed twice.

- Planning for College – how to fund your children's college education. Read the many different ideas in this chapter which includes the availability of financial aid packages. The chart shows which colleges to choose and guides you towards a prudent decision.

- Increase Your Income - Make more money in your spare time with these ideas. When you read the money-making ideas in this chapter, you will scratch your head and say, "why didn't I think of that?"

- Create a Document Storage and Retrieval System – So simple yet so effective. It will free up a lot of your limited living space.

- Stress-Free Personal Time Management – This system will organize your day and free up plenty of your time for use at your leisure.

- How to Store and Safeguard Passwords – Simple trick will help you create and remember strong passwords.

- How to maximize your Social Security benefits – In light of the elimination of "File and Suspend" and "Restricted Application" strategies, the chart shows claiming strategies for 1) Single never married, 2) currently married, 3) married at least 10 years, divorced at least 2 years, currently single, 4) divorced, has remarried and currently married, 5) widow/widower, 6) surviving divorced spouse, married at least 10 years, currently single or remarried after the age of 60.

- Best places for retirement – Some of these retirement communities are surprising. Some viable locations have ½ the cost of living of most cities in the U.S.

- Paying for Nursing Home and Long-Term Care

- How to qualify for Medicaid benefits for LTC
- How to reduce income to qualify for Medicaid

- How to reduce assets to qualify for Medicaid.

- Estate Planning – How to protect your estate from estate tax and inheritance tax.

- Enrich Your Life by Exploring the World – Travel as soon as you can while you are still young. This chapter discusses why the money you spend traveling and exploring the world is money well spent.

- **Staying Healthy and Fit as You Age** – There are a few minor behavior modification changes that you can put into practice that will keep you healthy throughout your retirement years.

- **Live a Rich, Happy, Healthy, Simple and Balanced Life**

- **Learn more, click on the link below:**

https://www.amazon.com/Living-Rich-Loving-healthy-balanced-ebook/dp/B01GORIB4Y/ref=pd_sim_sbs_351_2?ie=UTF8&psc=1&refRID=825N2SZCEYGWC1STH495

Excerpt from the book, *Living Rich & Loving It*:
Live a Rich, Happy, Healthy, Simple and Balanced Life

    Life does not have to be complicated. If you succeed in following the life strategies in this book, your children will end up well, your investments will provide you with a nice retirement nest egg that will last for as long as you live, you will minimize stress in your life and you will have more time for leisure and for activities that help keep your mind and body healthy. This book is not the magic bullet for success but a playbook to improve your odds for achieving success. There will be unexpected twists and turns in your life but the principles and strategies in this book will help lead you to the correct path to success and keep you on track to achieve all you want in life. If you have goals, dreams and aspirations in life, you have a sense of direction but you still need a road map to take you from here to there. I hope this book will serve as that road map for you.

Having a balanced life for me does not only mean having equal portions of work, play and family life. For me, it does not only mean having a sound mind, body and spirit. What I believe is that it is within us to muster the forces of nature to be on our side by reforming our own behavior in order to achieve a well-balanced life. If you do "the right thing", the right thing will come back to you. This is not necessarily karma but the realization that there is positive and negative energy in the universe that is out of our control and beyond our comprehension. Besides gravity and centrifugal force, there are forces in the universe we will never comprehend---frequencies, vibrations, fields of energy, our life force energy that affect people around us. I believe that doing the right thing will harness and call on all these forces to rally behind us. If it won't take too much effort on our part, why not choose to do the right thing? In doing so, I believe we will achieve the unity of mind, body, emotion and spirit which will awaken the genius in us. It is combining the fundamental rules of life with common sense, with the sum of our knowledge and with the unexplainable power of the universe............

Supplemental Disclaimer

The information contained in this book is provided to you "AS IS" and does not constitute legal or financial advice. All sample forms are for educational purposes only. We make no claims, promises or guarantees about the accuracy, completeness, or any specific result from the use of the contents or adequacy of the information contained in this book. Information contained in this book should not be used as substitute for obtaining financial and tax advice from a competent and licensed financial advisor and/or legal advice from an attorney licensed or authorized to practice in your jurisdiction. Medical or health information written in this book must not be misconstrued as medical advice. Consult your doctor or other healthcare provider before acting on any information provided in this book. Narratives in this book are based on true events.

No warranties are made regarding the suitability of this book. This book contains an accumulation of information based on the personal experience of the author. Prior results do not guarantee a similar outcome. The author and publisher do not guarantee the accuracy, completeness, efficacy and timeliness of the information provided herein. The information may no longer be current at the time of publication of this book. The reader should seek the advice of a licensed professional before acting on any information provided herein.

Various advice in this book do not take into account your objectives, financial situation or needs. Before acting on any advice you should consider the appropriateness of the advice and its applicability to your current situation. Any products mentioned in this book may not be appropriate for you. Product Disclosure Statements for those products must be requested and reviewed before making any decisions. We make no claims, promises or guarantees about the accuracy, completeness, or any specific result from the use of the contents or adequacy of the information contained in this book. The author and publisher and their affiliates, parents, subsidiaries, assigns, officers, directors, shareholders, employees, representatives, agents and servants assume no responsibility to any person who relies on information contained herein and disclaim all liability in respect to such information.

www.ingramcontent.com/pod-product-compliance
Lightning Source LLC
Chambersburg PA
CBHW031547210526
45464CB00003B/1188